PIANO FUN
FOLK SONGS AND SPIRITUALS
FOR ADULT BEGINNERS

Arranged by Brenda Dillon

Orchestrations by Will Baily

Speed • Pitch • Balance • Loop

To access audio, visit:
www.halleonard.com/mylibrary

Enter Code
3761-5124-4224-3454

ISBN 978-1-4950-5334-4

7777 W. BLUEMOUND RD. P.O. BOX 13819 MILWAUKEE, WI 53213

In Australia Contact:
Hal Leonard Australia Pty. Ltd.
4 Lentara Court
Cheltenham, Victoria, 3192 Australia
Email: ausadmin@halleonard.com.au

Visit Hal Leonard Online at
www.halleonard.com

PERFORMANCE NOTES

Introduction

Welcome to *Piano Fun: Folk Songs and Spirituals,* a collection of lead sheets and arrangements for the beginning pianist who has learned how to read music and wants to play easy arrangements of familiar melodies.

About the Orchestrations

Each orchestration has two tracks: a slow track and a slightly faster track. The orchestrator is Will Baily, composer and Recreational Music Making (RMM) facilitator who has been composing and orchestrating specifically for RMM students of all ages for the past seven years. He has presented at the MTNA conference and on MTNA's Pedagogy Saturday. A former college professor, Will operates a RMM studio in Scottsbluff, Nebraska that serves approximately 300 students of all ages.

Compositional Variety

Although this book doesn't include original compositions, it does feature compositional variety in the arrangements. *Piano Teacher's Guide to Creative Composition* by Carol Klose provides several excellent ideas, including how to develop interesting accompaniments and add spice to chord progressions.

In addition to unusual chord choices, these arrangements include the following compositional techniques to create variety:

Ritardando (rit.) – gradually slowing down which often occurs at the end of the song, but can also be used in other places to create musical feeling.

Grace note – a small note which is played immediately before the main note and does not add or take away value from that note. The smaller note often has a slash through the stem.

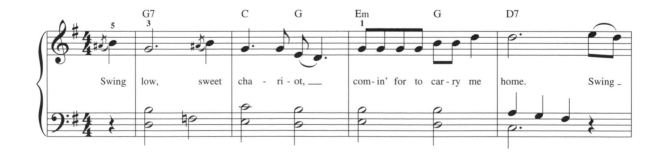

Syncopation – occurs when the normal or expected pattern of rhythm shifts from a strong beat to a weak beat or a weak part of a beat, and sometimes includes a tie. In 4/4 time signature the first beat is strong, the 3rd beat is less strong and the 2nd and 4th beats are weak. In 3/4 time the 1st beat is strong and the 2nd and 3rd beats are weak.

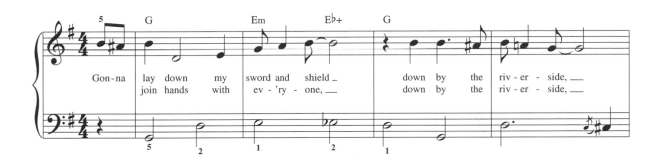

Modulation – a change of key within a composition that sometimes is signaled by a "pivot chord."

"Nobody Knows the Trouble I've Seen" (page 32) begins with a key signature of one sharp. However, measures 25-36 have a key signature of one flat. The chord in measure 24 that signaled the change is a C7 chord, which has a B-flat.

– Brenda Dillon

LEAD SHEETS

Deep River

African-American Spiritual
Based on Joshua 3
Arranged by Brenda Dillon

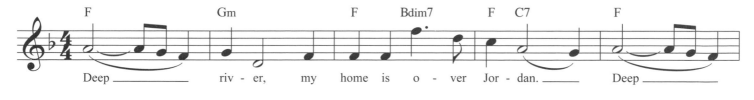

Deep _____ riv - er, my home is o - ver Jor - dan. _____ Deep _____

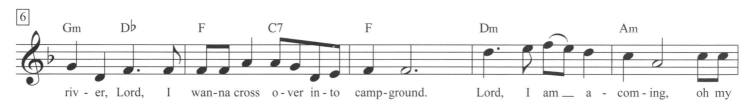

riv - er, Lord, I wan-na cross o - ver in - to camp-ground. Lord, I am __ a - com - ing, oh my

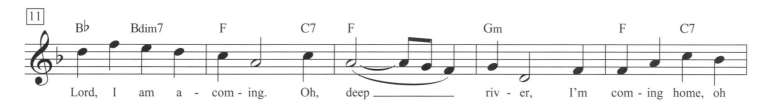

Lord, I am a - com - ing. Oh, deep _____ riv - er, I'm com - ing home, oh

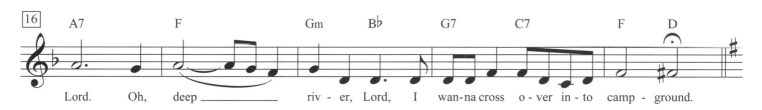

Lord. Oh, deep _____ riv - er, Lord, I wan-na cross o - ver in - to camp - ground.

Deep _____ riv - er, my home is o - ver Jor - dan. _____ Deep _____

riv - er, Lord, I wan-na cross o - ver in - to camp-ground. Lord, I am __ a - com - ing, oh my

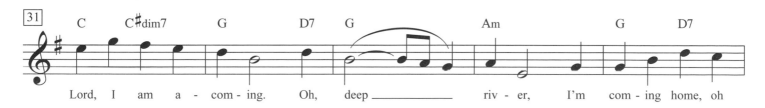

Lord, I am a - com - ing. Oh, deep _____ riv - er, I'm com - ing home, oh

Lord. Oh, deep _____ riv - er, Lord, I wan-na cross o - ver in - to camp-ground.
rit.

Down by the Riverside

African-American Spiritual
Arranged by Brenda Dillon

Go, Tell It on the Mountain

African-American Spiritual
Verses by John W. Work, Jr.
Arranged by Brenda Dillon

I've Got Peace Like a River

Traditional
Arranged by Brenda Dillon

Jacob's Ladder

African-American Spiritual
Arranged by Brenda Dillon

My Lord, What a Morning

African-American Spiritual
Arranged by Brenda Dillon

Nobody Knows the Trouble I've Seen

African-American Spiritual
Arranged by Brenda Dillon

Rock-a-My Soul

African-American Spiritual
Arranged by Brenda Dillon

Shenandoah

American Folksong
Arranged by Brenda Dillon

Steal Away

(Steal Away to Jesus)

Traditional Spiritual
Arranged by Brenda Dillon

Swing Low, Sweet Chariot

Traditional Spiritual
Arranged by Brenda Dillon

15

Water Is Wide/Wade in the Water

Traditional
Arranged by Brenda Dillon

Wayfaring Stranger

Southern American Folk Hymn
Arranged by Brenda Dillon

Were You There?/Kum Ba Yah

Traditional Spiritual
Harmony by Charles Winfred Douglas
Arranged by Brenda Dillon

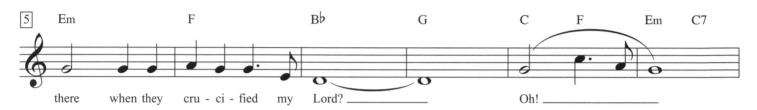

Were you there when they cru-ci-fied my Lord? _____ Were you

there when they cru-ci-fied my Lord? _____ Oh! _____

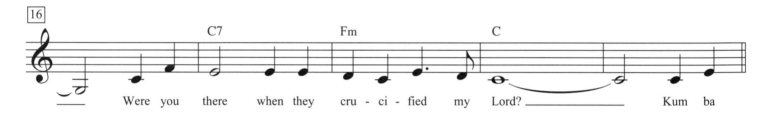

Some-times it caus-es me to trem-ble, trem-ble, trem-ble. _____

_____ Were you there when they cru-ci-fied my Lord? _____ Kum ba

Kum Ba Yah
Traditional Spiritual

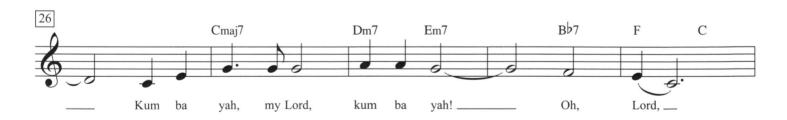

yah, my Lord, kum ba yah! _____ Kum ba yah, my Lord, kum ba yah! _____

_____ Kum ba yah, my Lord, kum ba yah! _____ Oh, Lord, _____

kum ba yah! _____ Come by here, come by here, come by here. Oh, _ Lord.

rit.

ARRANGEMENTS

Deep River

African-American Spiritual
Based on Joshua 3
Arranged by Brenda Dillon

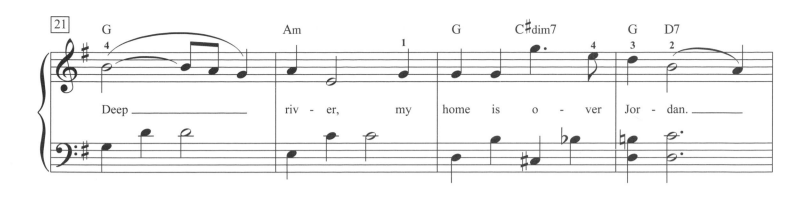

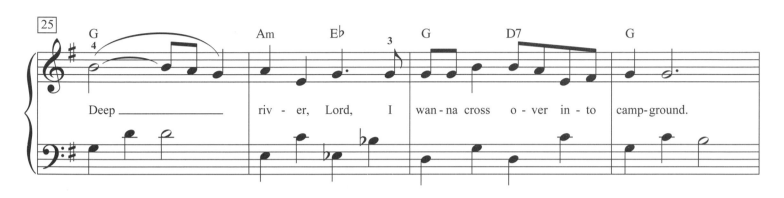

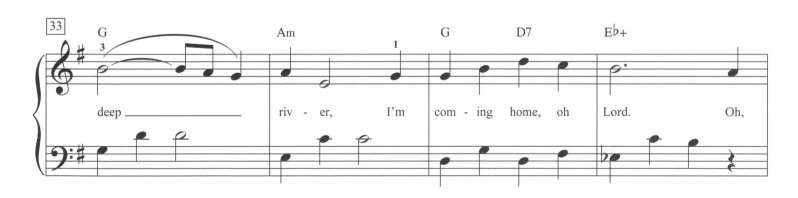

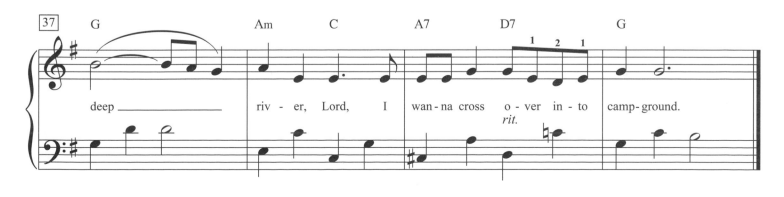

Down by the Riverside

African-American Spiritual
Arranged by Brenda Dillon

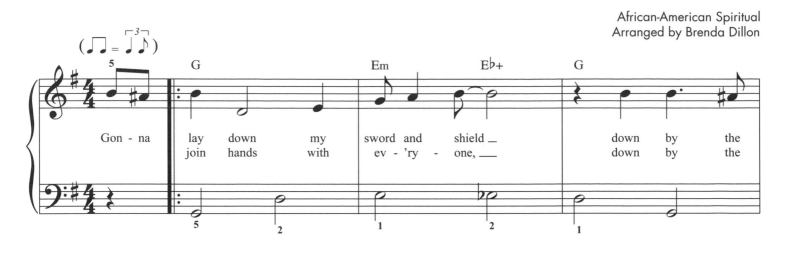

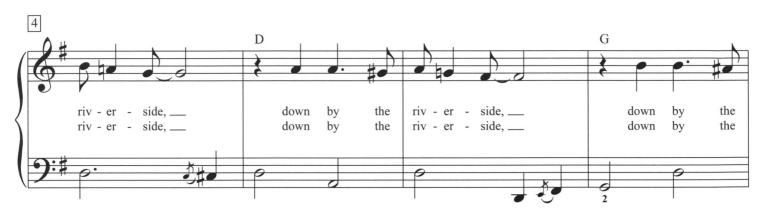

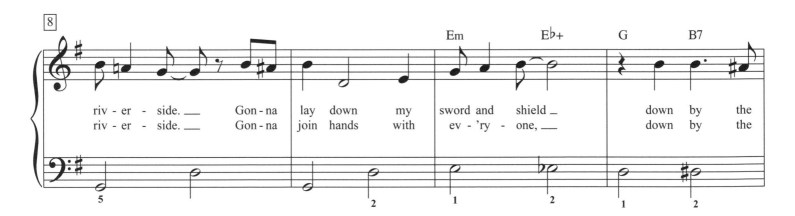

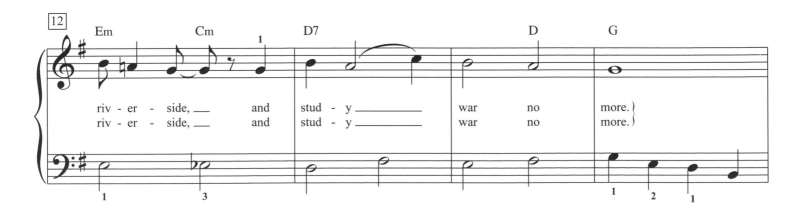

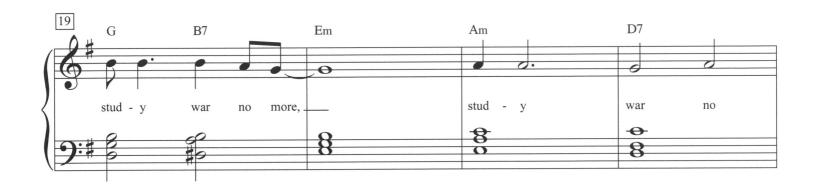

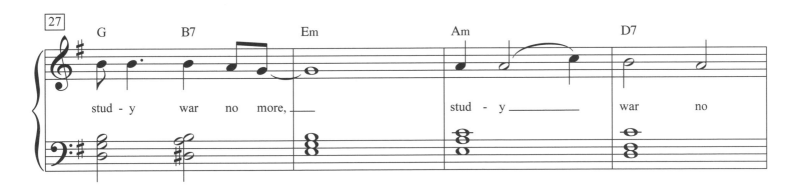

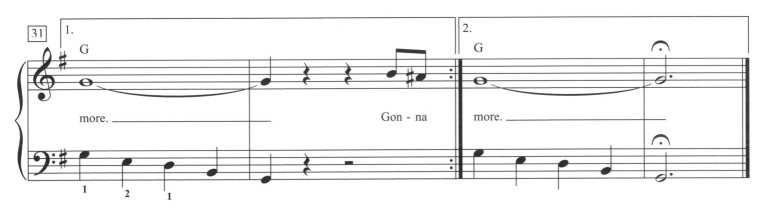

Go, Tell It on the Mountain

African-American Spiritual
Verses by John W. Work, Jr.
Arranged by Brenda Dillon

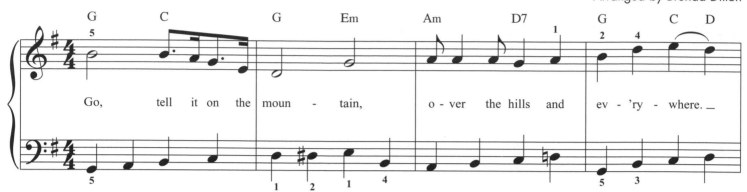

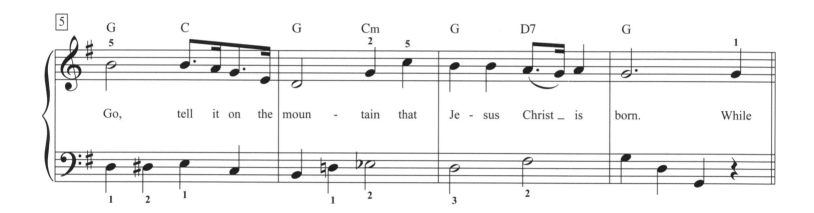

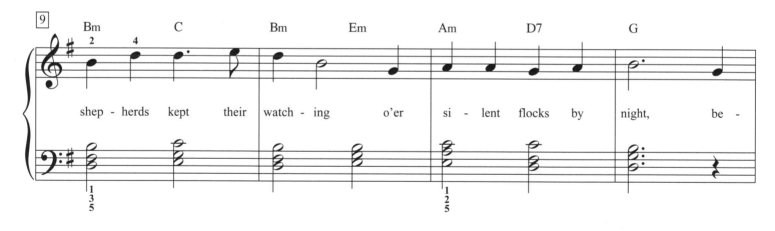

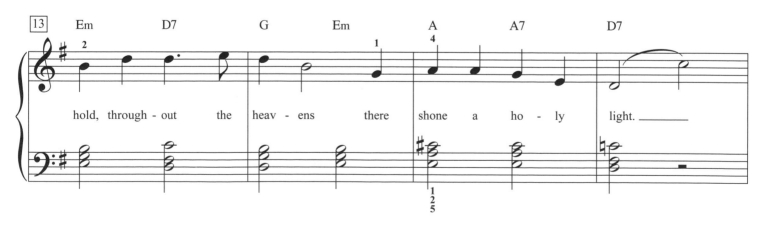

25

I've Got Peace Like a River

Traditional
Arranged by Brenda Dillon

Jacob's Ladder

African-American Spiritual
Arranged by Brenda Dillon

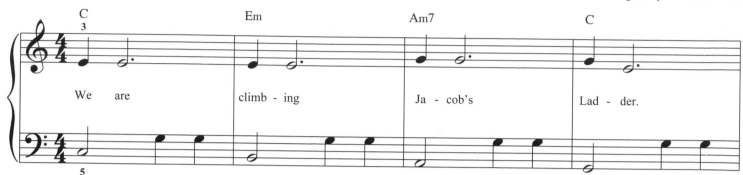

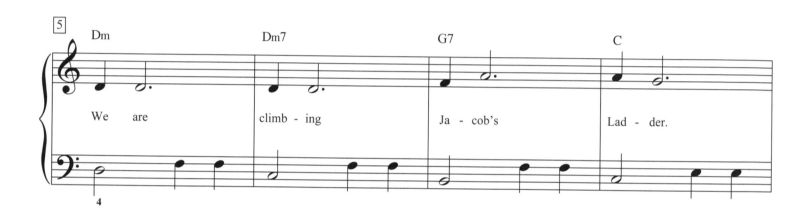

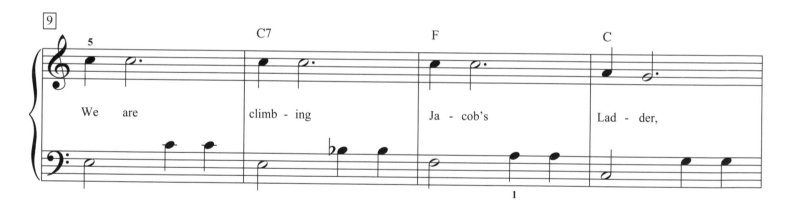

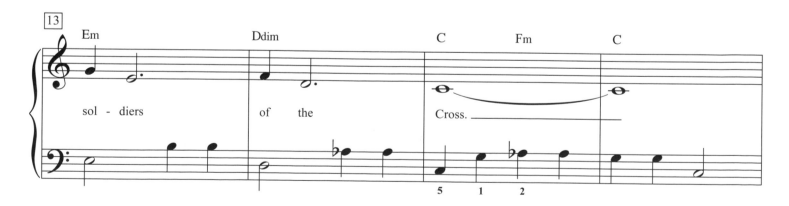

29

My Lord, What a Morning

African-American Spiritual
Arranged by Brenda Dillon

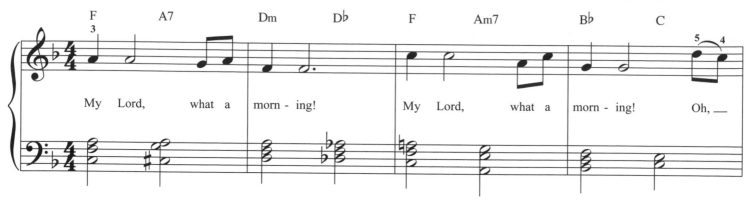

30

Nobody Knows the Trouble I've Seen

African-American Spiritual
Arranged by Brenda Dillon

Rock-a-My Soul

African-American Spiritual
Arranged by Brenda Dillon

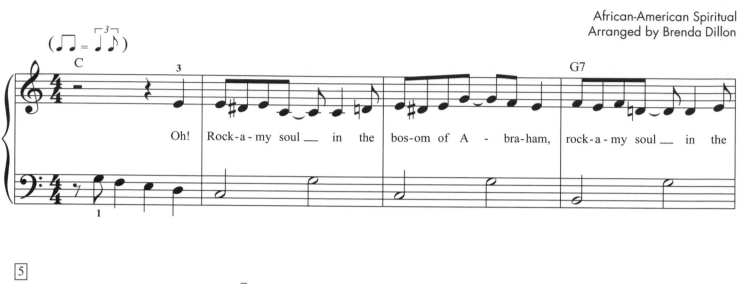

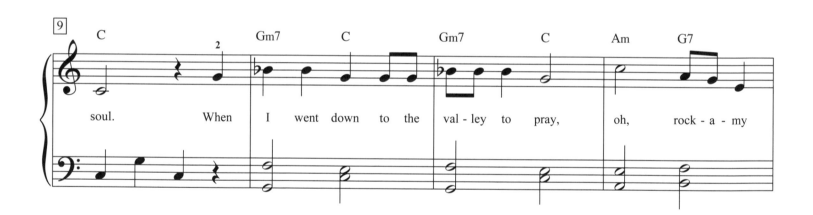

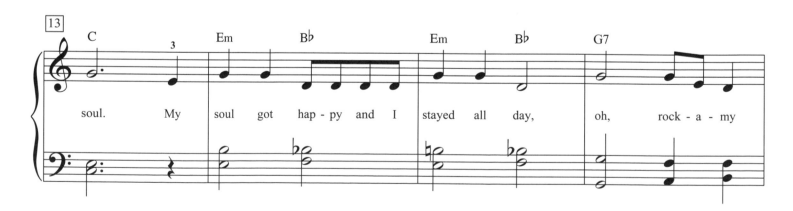

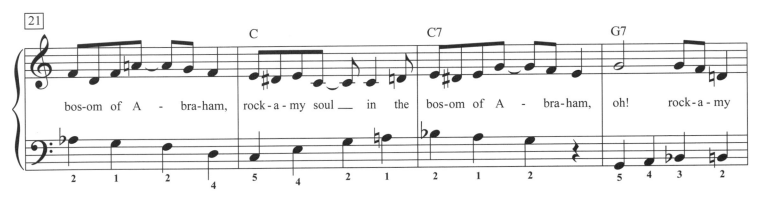

35

Shenandoah

American Folksong
Arranged by Brenda Dillon

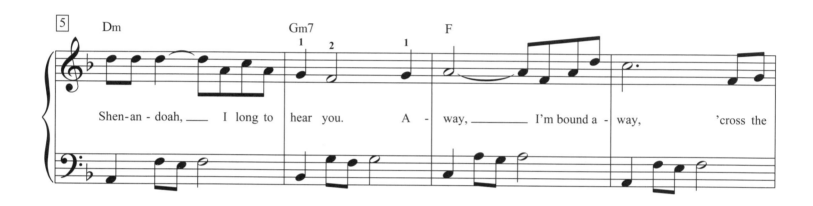

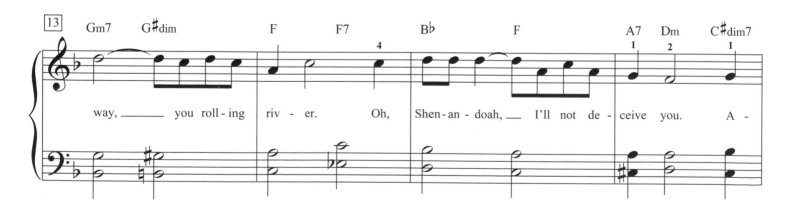

Steal Away

(Steal Away to Jesus)

Traditional Spiritual
Arranged by Brenda Dillon

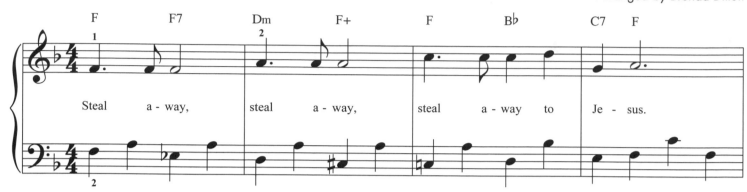

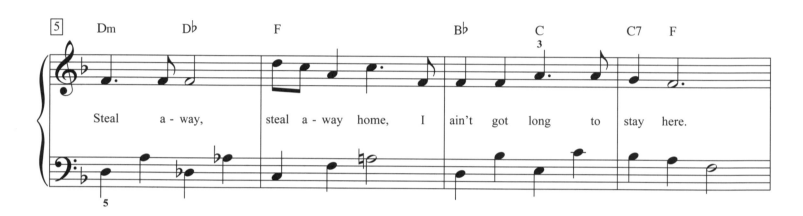

Steal a - way, steal a - way, steal a - way to Je - sus.

Steal a - way, steal a - way home, I ain't got long to stay here.

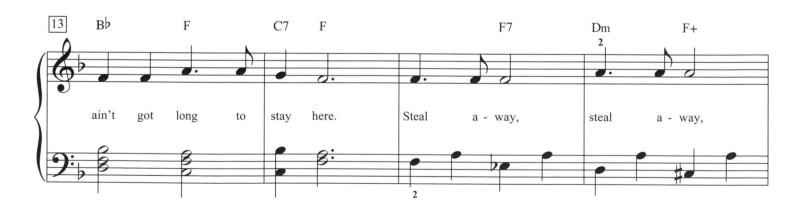

My Lord, He calls me, He calls me by the thun-der. The trum-pet sounds with - in ___ my soul, I

ain't got long to stay here. Steal a - way, steal a - way,

Swing Low, Sweet Chariot

Traditional Spiritual
Arranged by Brenda Dillon

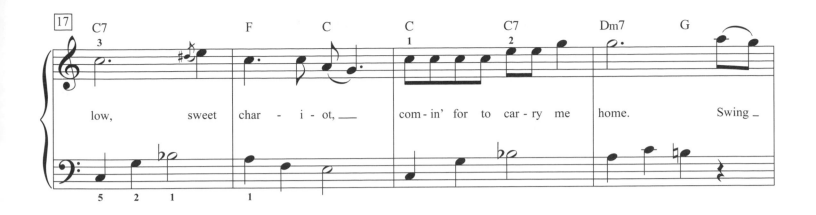

low, sweet char - i - ot, ___ com - in' for to car - ry me home. Swing ___

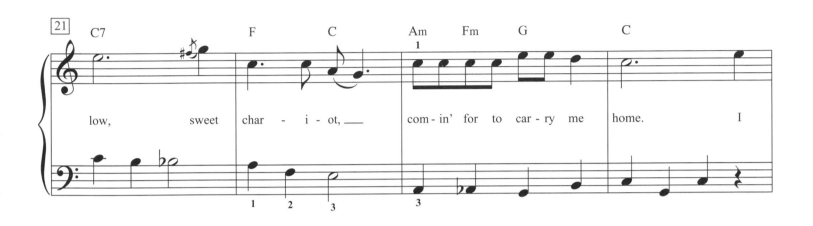

low, sweet char - i - ot, ___ com - in' for to car - ry me home. I

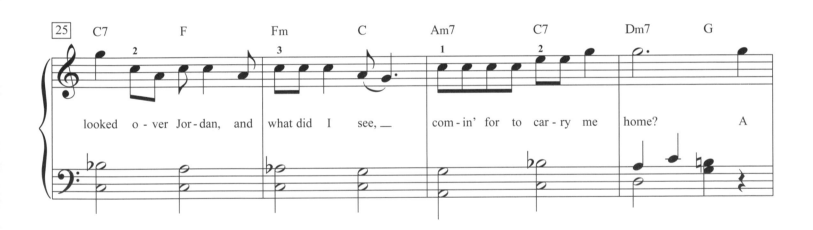

looked o - ver Jor - dan, and what did I see, ___ com - in' for to car - ry me home? A

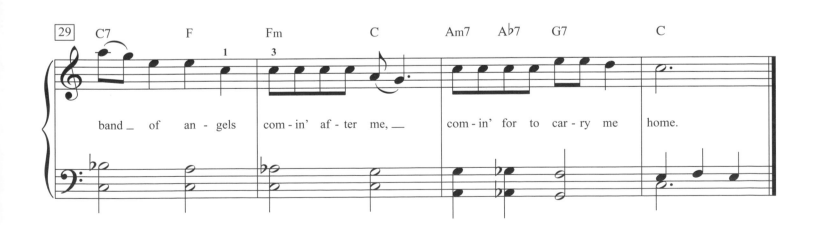

band ___ of an - gels com - in' af - ter me, ___ com - in' for to car - ry me home.

Water Is Wide/Wade in the Water

Traditional
Arranged by Brenda Dillon

Wade in the Water

Traditional Spiritual

43

Wayfaring Stranger

Southern American Folk Hymn
Arranged by Brenda Dillon

Were You There?/Kum Ba Yah

Traditional Spiritual
Harmony by Charles Winfred Douglas
Arranged by Brenda Dillon

Were you there when they cru-ci-fied my Lord? _____ Were you

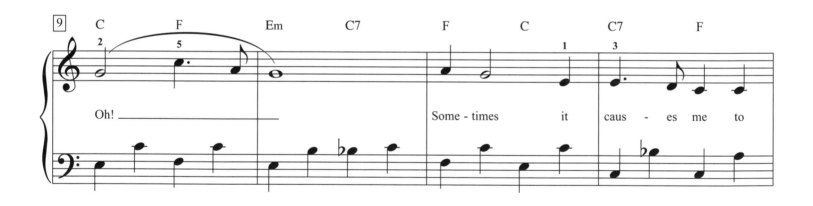

there when they cru-ci-fied my Lord? _____

Oh! _____ Some-times it caus-es me to

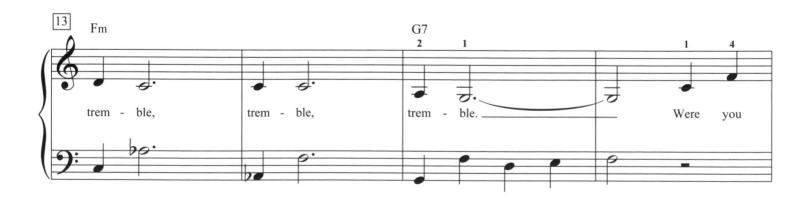

trem-ble, trem-ble, trem-ble. _____ Were you

Kum Ba Yah
Traditional Spiritual

Hal Leonard Student Piano Library

Adult Piano Method

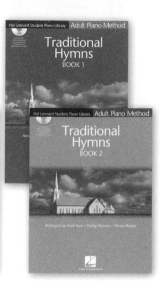

Adult Piano Method

Adults want to play rewarding music and enjoy their piano study. They deserve a method that lives up to those expectations. The *Hal Leonard Student Piano Library Adult Piano Method* does just that and more.

Method Book 1
00296441 Book/Online Audio $16.99

Method Book 2
00296480 Book/Online Audio $16.99

Popular Hits Book 1

Our hit-packed supplementary songbook includes these titles: American Pie • Circle of Life • Fun, Fun, Fun • Let It Be Me • Murder, She Wrote • The Music of the Night • My Heart Will Go On • Sing • Strangers in the Night • Vincent (Starry Starry Night) • Y.M.C.A. • The Way You Look Tonight.

00296541 Book/Online Audio $12.99

Popular Hits Book 2

12 hits: I Will Remember You • I Wish You Love • I Write the Songs • In the Mood • Moon River • Oh, Pretty Woman • The Phantom of the Opera • Stand by Me • Tears in Heaven • Unchained Melody • What a Wonderful World • When I'm Sixty-Four.

00296652 Book/Online Audio $12.99

Popular Favorites Book 1

11 favorites: Are You Lonesome Tonight? • Bless the Broken Road • Don't Know Why • Every Breath You Take • From a Distance • Help Me Make It Through the Night • I Hope You Dance • Imagine • Lean on Me • The Nearness of You • Right Here Waiting.

00296826 Book/Enhanced CD Pack...$12.99

Popular Favorites Book 2

12 classics: All I Have to Do Is Dream • Georgia on My Mind • I Just Called to Say I Love You • I'm a Believer • Memory • Never on a Sunday • On My Own • One Fine Day • Satin Doll • That'll Be the Day • We Are the World • Your Song.

00296842 Book/Enhanced CD Pack...$12.99

Christmas Favorites Book 1

12 favorites: Away in a Manger • Deck the Hall • God Rest Ye Merry, Gentlemen • I Saw Three Ships • Jingle Bells • Joy to the World • O Come, O Come, Emmanuel • O Little Town of Bethleham • Silent Night • Ukrainian Bell Carol • We Wish You a Merry Christmas • What Child Is This?

00296544 Book/CD Pack...$12.99

Christmas Favorites Book 2

12 more holiday classics: Angels We Have Heard on High • Bring a Torch, Jeannette Isabella • Dance of the Sugar Plum Fairy • Ding Dong! Merrily on High! • The First Noel • Go, Tell It on the Mountain • Hark! The Herald Angels Sing • The Holly and the Ivy • O Christmas Tree • O Holy Night • Still, Still, Still • We Three Kings of Orient Are.

00296668 Book/CD Pack...$12.99

Traditional Hymns Book 1

16 sacred favorites: All Glory, Laud and Honor • Come, Thou Almighty King • For the Beauty of the Earth • Holy, Holy, Holy! • It Is Well with My Soul • Joyful, Joyful, We Adore Thee • A Mighty Fortress Is Our God • What a Friend We Have in Jesus • and more.

00296782 Book/CD Pack...$12.99

Traditional Hymns Book 2

15 more traditional hymns: All Things Bright and Beautiful • Ezekiel Saw the Wheel • God of Grace and God of Glory • God Will Take Care of You • In the Garden • Lord, I Want to Be a Christian • Stand Up, Stand Up for Jesus • Swing Low, Sweet Chariot • This Is My Father's World • and more.

00296783 Book/CD Pack...$12.99

Prices, contents and availability are subject to change without notice.

FOR MORE INFORMATION, SEE YOUR LOCAL MUSIC DEALER, OR WRITE TO:

HAL•LEONARD® CORPORATION

7777 W. BLUEMOUND RD. P.O. BOX 13819 MILWAUKEE, WI 53213

www.halleonard.com